T0390228

Desert
Plants and Animals

THIS EDITION
Editorial Management by Oriel Square
Produced for DK by WonderLab Group LLC
Jennifer Emmett, Erica Green, Kate Hale, *Founders*

Editors Grace Hill Smith, Libby Romero, Maya Myers, Michaela Weglinski;
Photography Editors Kelley Miller, Annette Kiesow, Nicole DiMella;
Managing Editor Rachel Houghton; **Designers** Project Design Company;
Researcher Michelle Harris; **Copy Editor** Lori Merritt; **Indexer** Connie Binder;
Proofreader Larry Shea; **Reading Specialist** Dr. Jennifer Albro; **Curriculum Specialist** Elaine Larson

Published in the United States by DK Publishing
1745 Broadway, 20th Floor, New York, NY 10019

Copyright © 2023 Dorling Kindersley Limited
DK, a Division of Penguin Random House LLC
23 24 25 26 10 9 8 7 6 5 4 3 2 1
001-333893-Oct/2023

A catalog record for this book
is available from the Library of Congress.
HC ISBN: 978-0-7440-7184-9
PB ISBN: 978-0-7440-7187-0

DK books are available at special discounts when purchased in bulk for sales promotions, premiums, fundraising, or educational use. For details, contact: DK Publishing Special Markets,
1745 Broadway, 20th Floor, New York, NY 10019
SpecialSales@dk.com

Printed and bound in China

The publisher would like to thank the following for their kind permission to reproduce their images:
a=above; c=center; b=below; l=left; r=right; t=top; b/g=background

Alamy Stock Photo: Norma Joseph 14b, Nature Picture Library / Bruno D'Amicis 28-29;
Dreamstime.com: Rinus Baak 12crb, Dianneslotten 26-27, Ecophoto 10-11, Frank Fichtmueller 11br, Aleksandr Frolov 20b, Hin255 11crb, Erika Kirkpatrick 1b, Kmitu 6-7, Luligu 15bl, Simone Matteo Giuseppe Manzoni / Jeppo75 4-5, Alex Petelin 12-13, Raymond Shiu 15br, 30clb, David Steele 30cl, Abdelmoumen Taoutaou 20-21, Joao Virissimo 30tl (bl), Jan Martin Will 24tr, Andrea Willmore 12bl, Willtu 24-25, Yulan 9cra, 30cla; **Getty Images:** Thomas Roche 16-17;
Getty Images / iStock: 2630ben 18-19; **naturepl.com:** Klein & Hubert 3cb, 22-23;
Shutterstock.com: Matt Makes Photos 8-9, Charles T. Peden 26b

Cover images: *Front:* **Dreamstime.com:** Annaav b; **Shutterstock.com:** Nyuanjit;
Back: **Dreamstime.com:** Mstjahanara903 bl

All other images © Dorling Kindersley
For more information see: www.dkimages.com

For the curious
www.dk.com

Level

1

Desert
Plants and Animals

Libby Romero

Contents

What Is a Desert?

Which things are true?
Deserts are hot.
Deserts are cold.
Many things
live in deserts.
All of these things
are true!

There are different
kinds of deserts.
Some deserts are sandy.
Some deserts are rocky.
Some deserts are
full of ice.

All deserts are alike
in one way.
All deserts are dry.

Even though they are dry, deserts are full of life. Plants grow in deserts. Animals live in deserts.

These plants and animals have adaptations.
An adaptation is a change in a living thing.
Adaptations help living things survive wherever they are ... even in deserts!

Desert Plants

Desert plants are amazing.
Their adaptations
are amazing, too!
These flowers grow
in the desert.
They wait for rain.
When it rains,
they bloom fast.

The flowers spread
their seeds.
The seeds wait and wait.
Finally, it rains again.
New flowers grow fast!

Antarctica is a very
cold desert.
Sometimes, it is dark
all day long.
Antarctic moss is short.
It needs very little light.
When it is cold and icy,
the moss dries itself out.
When the ice melts,
it takes in water again.

This cactus grows in a hot desert. The cactus gets lots of light. Its hairy spines are leaves! The spines block sunlight. They keep the cactus cool.

spines

Desert plants do not
need a lot of rain.
This kind of cactus
has a big, waxy stem.
The stem swells
to store water.
Wax seals the water in.

The cactus has
many roots.
Most of the
roots are shallow.
One root grows
straight down.
It reaches the water
deeper underground.

stem

This plant looks
like a tree.
A white powder
covers its branches.

branches

The branches reflect
the sun's heat.
The plant stays cool.

Sometimes, it is too dry.
The plant needs water.
Its branches fall off!
After it rains, they
grow back.

Desert Animals

Deserts are full of animals.
The animals have different
kinds of adaptations.
They are built to survive in
different kinds of deserts.

Camels live in hot deserts.
It is hard to find
plants to eat there.
But camels store fat
in their humps.
The fat breaks down and
gives the camels energy.

Jerboas are tiny.
But they jump
high and far.
This helps them escape
from other animals that
want to eat them.

Jerboas have big ears.
Heat goes out their ears.
This helps keep
them cool.

Penguins have thick feathers. They have fat called blubber.
The feathers and blubber help them stay warm.

These penguins
work together.
They form a big group.
They move around.
No penguins are left
alone in the cold.

This tortoise gets some of the water it needs from the plants it eats. It can go a long time between drinks.

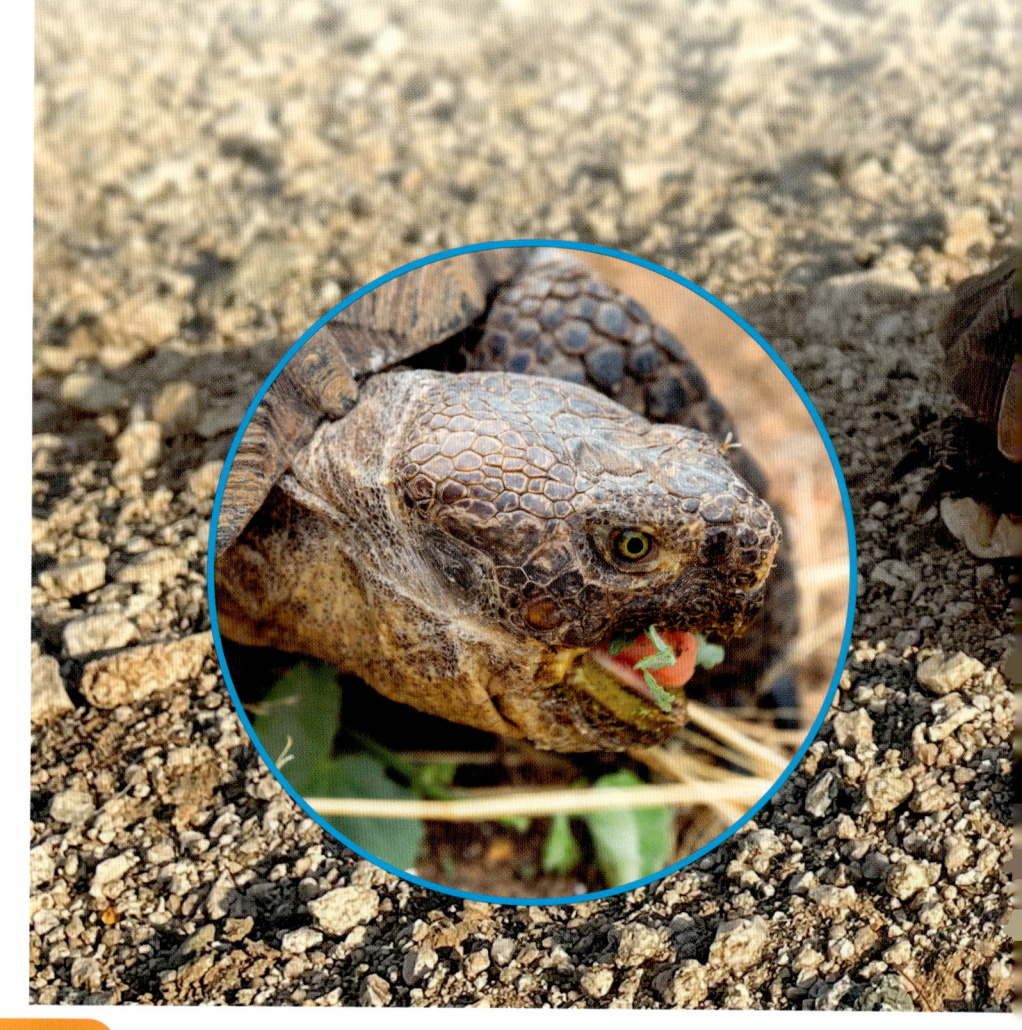

The tortoise stores water in its bladder. Its body uses the water later on.

Living in a desert is hard.
But plants do it.
Animals do, too.

The desert is their home.
They are built to
survive here.

Glossary

adaptation
a change that helps a plant or animal survive where it lives

desert
an area of dry land with few plants and little rain or snow

reflect
to bounce back light

spine
a hard, pointed leaf of a cactus

stem
the main part or stalk of a plant

Index

Quiz

Answer the questions to see what you have learned. Check your answers with an adult.

1. How are all deserts alike?

2. Which part of a cactus swells and stores water?

3. What is a camel's hump filled with?

4. What are three adaptations that help penguins in Antarctica stay warm?

5. What is your favorite desert plant or animal? What adaptations help it survive in the desert?

1. They are dry 2. The stem 3. Fat
4. Feathers, blubber, and huddling together in a group
5. Answers will vary